THE BAHÁ'Í FAITH AND LIFE AFTER DEATH

Andrew Mancey

These books are dedicated to the memory of my mother and father who continue to inspire me. And to Moeen Kiani who gave me the idea.

Many thanks to the National Spiritual Assembly of the Bahá'ís of Guyana for their support.

PREFACE

The writer originally undertook this series in an attempt to put into ebook format some booklets published locally by a Bahá'í friend who recently passed away. One thing led to another, and with much learning along the way, here we are with the booklets on Kindle as a work still in progress. It is likely that the booklets will continue to be periodically revised, improved and perhaps expanded. The aim is always to provide introductory material about the Bahá'í Faith to a wide audience at a low price. And to encourage the reader to move on to more comprehensive resources.

1. INTRODUCTION

The Bahá'í Faith is the most recent of the world's major religions. It was founded by Bahá'u'lláh in the 1800's. Its main principle is the oneness of mankind, that humanity is one people with one origin with our planet as its home. It is established in more than 100,000 localities, in almost every country and territory around the world.

In this booklet we look at life after death and the teachings of the Bahá'í Faith on the subject. We start by considering briefly how western culture regards death and life after death. After looking at Bahá'í teachings on God and the soul, we look at the teachings on life after death and the nature of the next world.

We assume some basic knowledge of the Bahá'í Faith and its Founder, Bahá'u'lláh. Further information about the Faith can be found at the end of the booklet (Appendix A).

Many quotations from the Bahá'í Writings have been used in order to try and convey the teachings accurately. Additional explanations may be added which are just the opinion of the writer and have no authority.

Despite the number of quotations used, this is not a complete treatment of the subject and there is more to be found on this subject in the Bahá'í Writings. A few quotations may occur twice in the text. At the end of the booklet there is a list of relevant books for the interested reader.

2. IS THERE LIFE AFTER DEATH?

Belief in life after death has changed significantly over recent times. While the writer has not come across authoritative research on this, it would seem that for centuries the great majority of mankind followed one or other of the major religions and had a firm belief in a Supreme Being, and in some form of life after death. In the twentieth century, in the more wealthy parts of the world and in socialist countries, there has been a decline in such beliefs. More recently, however, there seems to have been increasing interest in the topic and in near-death experiences (see Appendix B).

All the Prophets and Manifestations of God taught that the soul continues on after death and Their lives demonstrate this belief. Bahá'u'lláh said:

> "Wert thou to ponder in thine heart the behavior of the Prophets of God thou wouldst assuredly and readily testify that there must needs be other worlds besides this world... How could such Souls have consented to surrender themselves unto their enemies if they believed all the worlds of God to have been reduced to this earthly life? Would they have willingly suffered such afflictions and torments as no man hath ever

experienced or witnessed?" [1]

Bahá'u'lláh has given us considerable knowledge about the soul and life after death as we shall see below. So for Bahá'ís there is no doubt about life after death and it becomes a source of reassurance in this life.

For Muslims and Christians their Holy Books are less clear and while life after death is affirmed, conflicting doctrines and beliefs have arisen.
We will look at further evidence for life after death below.

Why study life after death?

Investigating life after death often leads to a more positive and productive attitude to life. A materialistic attitude to life may lead to depression.

'Abdu'l-Bahá, the son of Bahá'u'lláh and designated Center of His Covenant, said:

> "When our thoughts are filled with the bitterness of this world, let us turn our eyes to the sweetness of God's compassion and He will send us heavenly calm! If we are imprisoned in the material world, our spirit can soar into the Heavens and we shall be free indeed!
> When our days are drawing to a close let us think of the eternal worlds, and we shall be full of joy!
> ... If your days on earth are numbered, you know that everlasting life awaits you. If material anxiety envelops you in a dark cloud, spiritual radiance lightens your path. Verily, those whose minds are illumined by the Spirit of the Most High have supreme consolation." [2]

> "A friend asked: "How should one look forward to death?"

'Abdu'l-Bahá answered: "How does one look forward to the goal of any journey? With hope and with expectation. It is even so with the end of this earthly journey. In the next world, man will find himself freed from many of the disabilities under which he now suffers." [3]

"O My servants! Sorrow not if, in these days and on this earthly plane, things contrary to your wishes have been ordained and manifested by God, for days of blissful joy, of heavenly delight, are assuredly in store for you." [4]

Knowing, believing in life after death changes our attitude to life. This is hardly surprising. Consider going on a journey when the destination was non-existent. Now consider if the destination was known to be a much-loved and happy place. Clearly our attitude during the journey would be quite different.

Disbelief in life after death is a part of a materialistic attitude to life common in wealthy countries today. According to a report of an interview put out by the American Psychological Association a materialistic attitude has negative effects:

"I think materialism is viewed in a negative light because people may have had unpleasant experiences with materialistic people. We know from research that materialism tends to be associated with treating others in more competitive, manipulative and selfish ways, as well as with being less empathetic. Such behavior is usually not appreciated by the average person, although it is encouraged by some aspects of our capitalist economic system."

"The research shows there is a tension between materialistic goals and religious pursuits, just as Jesus, Muhammad, Buddha, Lao Tze and many other religious thinkers have long suggested. It seems that trying to pursue materialistic and spiritual goals causes people conflict and stress, which in turn lowers their well-being." [5]

3. ATTITUDES TO DEATH

Let us take a closer look at attitudes to death.

According to Wikipedia:

> "Many people are afraid of dying. Discussing, thinking, or planning their own deaths causes them discomfort. This fear may cause them to put off financial planning, preparing a will and testament, or requesting help from a hospice organization." [6]

Consider, every day 150,000 people die[7] and enter the next world. Where do they all go? It is a well-traveled route and the next world (or worlds) must be vast indeed!

In the Bahá'í community it is the writer's experience that fear of death declines and disappears as we gain experience and knowledge. It is usual to say a prayer at a meeting if a friend has recently passed on and there are many prayers revealed for the departed. Bahá'í funerals have a strong spiritual atmosphere without strong displays of emotion. Death is not seen as the end but as a new beginning.

In recent years there has been increasing interest in what are called "Near-Death Experiences" (NDE), especially in the US. These are profound spiritual experiences which may occur while someone is near physical death such as during cardiac arrest. It has long been regarded as some kind of hallucination and not worthy of serious study. But many in the medical profession no longer dismiss it but accept it as a real occurrence. Some medical schools include it in their curriculum.

What we can note here is that those who do have an NDE also become convinced of the reality of life after death and also lose their fear of death. The experiences reported are largely in agreement with what the Bahá'í Writings portray.

In a study of some 300 cardiac patients, some of whom had an NDE, an "eight-year follow-up, people who had reported NDE generally did not show any fear of death and strongly believed in an afterlife, in contrast to people who had not reported NDE." [8]

An article in The Conversation put it like this:

"There is a widespread belief in Western cultures that death is the end, but many people who have had an NDE say this is not so – the feeling of having conscious awareness and existing outside of one's physical body suggests the self does not end."

"Recent large-scale studies conducted across the US, UK, Austria and Belgium have provided credible findings to suggest NDEs may actually be real phenomena. But the debate about the "realness" of NDEs is likely to continue for many years, if not decades, to come.

Whether they are verifiably real occurrences that can be scientifically quantified or not is, in many ways, irrelevant. What is significant is that people who have had NDEs universally report a complete loss of the most existential of human fears – something even the most advanced psychotherapies cannot achieve. People who have had an NDE don't wish for death. They want to live and fulfill their destiny. But when death finally calls, they will not be afraid. And that is quite extraordinary." [9]

These views expressed are from public and popular sources, not from Bahá'í sources. See Appendix B for further information on the Near-Death Experience (NDE) phenomenon.

We now look at what Bahá'u'lláh says about God and the way in which He guides mankind through His Manifestations. This will provide some necessary background before we see what He taught about life after death. See Appendix A for more on the Bahá'í Faith.

4. THE NATURE OF GOD

Bahá'u'lláh makes it very clear that there is only one God Who is exalted beyond all description or understanding.

> "To every discerning and illuminated heart it is evident that God, the unknowable Essence, the Divine Being, is immensely exalted beyond every human attribute, such as corporeal existence, ascent and descent, egress and regress. Far be it from His glory that human tongue should adequately recount His praise, or that human heart comprehend His fathomless mystery." [10]

> "O SON OF MAN!
> My majesty is My gift to thee, and My grandeur the token of My mercy unto thee. That which beseemeth Me none shall understand, nor can anyone recount. Verily, I have preserved it in My hidden storehouses and in the treasuries of My command, as a sign of My loving-kindness unto My servants and My mercy unto My people." [11]

God therefore sends His Manifestations (or Prophets) to teach us and to represent Him. Bahá'u'lláh stated:

> "These sanctified Mirrors, these Daysprings of ancient

glory are one and all the Exponents on earth of Him Who is the central Orb of the universe, its Essence and ultimate Purpose. From Him proceed their knowledge and power; from Him is derived their sovereignty. The beauty of their countenance is but a reflection of His image, and their revelation a sign of His deathless glory." [12]

The way in which God sends His Manifestations to mankind through the ages is referred to as 'progressive revelation'.

Progressive revelation

According to Bahá'u'lláh just as there is only one God, there is only one religion, God's religion. What some regard as different religions are like different chapters in the same book or different classes in one school.

God's divine Teachers (Manifestations of God) are sent with teachings suited for the needs of that time and place. This process is progressive and causes civilizations to advance through the ages. It is a process without end.

These Manifestations can be seen as being like mirrors. God is like the Sun. Each Mirror reflects the qualities of the Sun but the Sun is one. The Mirrors may vary in shape but it is the same Sun being reflected.

Thus, for example, Christ brought wonderful teachings which built on those of Moses and mankind advanced spiritually and materially. In this day we are in need of additional guidance because the needs of mankind are different, and its capacity has increased.

In times past Moses, Abraham, Buddha, Muhammad,

Zoroaster, Krishna and others were all sent by God. Others will come in the future.

Each Manifestation brings laws to guide us, teachings to educate us and an example of how to live and treat others. There is a spiritual component which always remains true such as the practice of virtues like truthfulness, love, patience, compassion, humility and equity. There is also a social component which changes to meet the needs of the age such as guidance for gatherings, fasting, diet, social organisation and so on. Bahá'u'lláh said:

> "Every one of them is the Way of God that connecteth this world with the realms above, and the Standard of His Truth unto every one in the kingdoms of earth and heaven. They are the Manifestations of God amidst men, the evidences of His Truth, and the signs of His glory." [13]

> "Unto the cities of all nations He hath sent His Messengers, Whom He hath commissioned to announce unto men tidings of the Paradise of His good pleasure, and to draw them nigh unto the Haven of abiding security, the Seat of eternal holiness and transcendent glory." [14]

Bahá'u'lláh said regarding His own mission:

> "By the righteousness of God, my Well-Beloved! I have never aspired after worldly leadership. My sole purpose hath been to hand down unto men that which I was bidden to deliver by God, the Gracious, the Incomparable, that it may detach them from all that pertaineth to this world, and cause them to attain such heights as neither the ungodly can conceive, nor the

froward imagine." [15]

5. THE PURPOSE OF LIFE

Today we hear many asking about the purpose of life. This is clearly explained in the Bahá'í Writings. The purpose of life, according to Bahá'u'lláh, is to know God and to worship God. One of the most widely used prayers, revealed by Bahá'u'lláh, starts with the line:

> "I bear witness, O my God, that Thou hast created me to know Thee and to worship Thee." [16]

Bahá'u'lláh explains that this capacity is unique to mankind:

> "From among all created things He hath singled out for His special favor the pure, the gem-like reality of man, and invested it with a unique capacity of knowing Him and of reflecting the greatness of His glory." [17]

And eternal life is a part of God's purpose for man:

> "... the purpose of Him Who is the Eternal Truth hath been to confer everlasting life upon all men, and ensure their security and peace..." [18]

The implication is clearly that learning to "to know God and to worship God" will lead to "everlasting life" for the individual and "security and peace" for mankind. He revealed this verse:

> "O SON OF SPIRIT!
> My first counsel is this: Possess a pure, kindly and radiant heart, that thine may be a sovereignty ancient, imperishable and everlasting." [19]

How is this to be achieved? The "Prophets and Messengers of God" are His Teachers for mankind. This is the way it has always been. Bahá'u'lláh explains:

> "The Prophets and Messengers of God have been sent down for the sole purpose of guiding mankind to the straight Path of Truth. The purpose underlying Their revelation hath been to educate all men, that they may, at the hour of death, ascend, in the utmost purity and sanctity and with absolute detachment, to the throne of the Most High." [20]

The things of this world are here for us to use but Bahá'u'lláh warns us not to set our affections on them as it will not benefit us in the end:

> "The world is but a show, vain and empty, a mere nothing, bearing the semblance of reality. Set not your affections upon it. Break not the bond that uniteth you with your Creator, and be not of those that have erred and strayed from His ways. Verily I say, the world is like the vapor in a desert, which the thirsty dreameth to be water and striveth after it with all his might, until when he cometh unto it, he findeth it to be mere illusion." [21]

And:

> "O SON OF BEING!
> Busy not thyself with this world, for with fire We test

the gold, and with gold We test Our servants." [22]

We will now examine more closely at what Bahá'u'lláh has said about the soul.

6. OUR SOUL

The human being is noble and spiritual. We have a rational and immortal soul which comes into being at conception and which enables us to think rationally and abstractly. The Bahá'í Writings tell us that we need to develop our soul with spiritual qualities in this world as our soul passes to spiritual worlds after death where these spiritual qualities are required.

Bahá'u'lláh revealed:

> "Thou hast asked Me concerning the nature of the soul. Know, verily, that the soul is a sign of God, a heavenly gem whose reality the most learned of men hath failed to grasp, and whose mystery no mind, however acute, can ever hope to unravel. It is the first among all created things to declare the excellence of its Creator, the first to recognize His glory, to cleave to His truth, and to bow down in adoration before Him. If it be faithful to God, it will reflect His light, and will, eventually, return unto Him. If it fail, however, in its allegiance to its Creator, it will become a victim to self and passion, and will, in the end, sink in their depths."

> "Verily I say, the human soul is, in its essence, one of the signs of God, a mystery among His mysteries. It is one of the mighty signs of the Almighty, the harbinger that proclaimeth the reality of all the worlds of God.

Within it lieth concealed that which the world is now utterly incapable of apprehending." [23]

And God speaking through Bahá'u'lláh in the Hidden Words revealed:

"O SON OF BEING!
With the hands of power I made thee and with the fingers of strength I created thee; and within thee have I placed the essence of My light. Be thou content with it and seek naught else, for My work is perfect and My command is binding. Question it not, nor have a doubt thereof..." [24]

'Abdu'l-Bahá explains that the soul is immortal, beyond physical qualities and is valued for spiritual qualities.

"The soul is not a combination of elements, it is not composed of many atoms, it is of one indivisible substance and therefore eternal. It is entirely out of the order of the physical creation; it is immortal!" [25]

"The truth is that God has endowed all humankind with intelligence and perception and has confirmed all as His servants and children; therefore, in the plan and estimate of God there is no distinction between male or female. The soul that manifests pure deeds and spiritual graces is most precious in His sight and nearer to Him in its attainments." [26]

The soul is connected to our body but is not inside it. It is not a physical thing that can be measured or confined. 'Abdu'l-Bahá compared the body with a mirror and the soul as a lamp being reflected in it:

"...the rational soul, or the human spirit, does not

subsist through this body by inherence—that is to say, it does not enter it; for inherence and entrance are characteristics of bodies, and the rational soul is sanctified above this. It never entered this body to begin with, that it should require, upon leaving it, some other abode. No, the connection of the spirit with the body is even as the connection of this lamp with a mirror. If the mirror is polished and perfected, the light of the lamp appears therein, and if the mirror is broken or covered with dust, the light remains concealed." [27]

In order to develop and acquire spiritual qualities effort is needed, but divine assistance is also essential. Bahá'u'lláh explains using the analogy of a light being reflected in a mirror. The mirror cannot by itself clean off the dust which dims the reflection. Nor can a lamp light itself.

"These energies with which the Daystar of Divine bounty and Source of heavenly guidance hath endowed the reality of man lie, however, latent within him, even as the flame is hidden within the candle and the rays of light are potentially present in the lamp. The radiance of these energies may be obscured by worldly desires even as the light of the sun can be concealed beneath the dust and dross which cover the mirror. Neither the candle nor the lamp can be lighted through their own unaided efforts, nor can it ever be possible for the mirror to free itself from its dross." [28]

'Abdu'l-Bahá again uses the analogy of the mirror explains how we discover the reality of things:

"The human spirit, which distinguishes man from the animal, is the rational soul, and these two terms —the human spirit and the rational soul—designate one and the same thing. This spirit, which in the terminology of the philosophers is called the rational soul, encompasses all things and as far as human capacity permits, discovers their realities and becomes aware of the properties and effects, the characteristics and conditions of earthly things. But the human spirit, unless it be assisted by the spirit of faith, cannot become acquainted with the divine mysteries and the heavenly realities. It is like a mirror which, although clear, bright, and polished, is still in need of light. Not until a sunbeam falls upon it can it discover the divine mysteries." [29]

We will now look at some other issues related to our spiritual development in this world, such as tests, and what we need to focus on by way of preparation.

7. CHOICES WE MAKE

God allows us to choose our path but we are accountable for what we choose. By experiencing the consequences of our actions, we learn and grow. Bahá'u'lláh wrote:

> "And now, concerning thy question regarding the creation of man. Know thou that all men have been created in the nature made by God, the Guardian, the Self-Subsisting. Unto each one hath been prescribed a preordained measure, as decreed in God's mighty and guarded Tablets. All that which ye potentially possess can, however, be manifested only as a result of your own volition." [30]

> "For every act performed there shall be a recompense according to the estimate of God, and unto this the very ordinances and prohibitions prescribed by the Almighty amply bear witness. For surely if deeds were not rewarded and yielded no fruit, then the Cause of God—exalted is He—would prove futile. Immeasurably high is He exalted above such blasphemies! However, unto them that are rid of all attachments a deed is, verily, its own reward." [31]

When we are deciding what to do it is our spirit, not our ego, which can advise us. 'Abdu'l-Bahá explains:

"When you wish to reflect upon or consider a matter, you consult something within you. You say, shall I do it, or shall I not do it? Is it better to make this journey or abandon it? Whom do you consult? Who is within you deciding this question? Surely there is a distinct power, an intelligent ego. Were it not distinct from your ego, you would not be consulting it. It is greater than the faculty of thought. It is your spirit which teaches you, which advises and decides upon matters." [32]

Some call this process of consulting our spirit 'intuition' or 'having a hunch'. It is important and something we need to practice.

Tests

While in this world we experience difficulties, tests and trials. By these we are able to become spiritually stronger and our hearts become more pure. Part of this is our struggle with our ego and our selfish desires.

By not dwelling on material difficulties but turning to the spiritual our path becomes easier. 'Abdu'l-Bahá said:

"All these examples are to show you that the trials which beset our every step, all our sorrow, pain, shame and grief, are born in the world of matter; whereas the spiritual Kingdom never causes sadness. A man living with his thoughts in this Kingdom knows perpetual joy. The ills all flesh is heir to do not pass him by, but they only touch the surface of his life, the depths are calm and serene."

"Today, humanity is bowed down with trouble, sorrow and grief, no one escapes; the world is wet with tears;

but, thank God, the remedy is at our doors. Let us turn our hearts away from the world of matter and live in the spiritual world! It alone can give us freedom! If we are hemmed in by difficulties we have only to call upon God, and by His great Mercy we shall be helped." [33]

He explains how trials come about. Some are the result of our own actions, some are sent by God to help us learn.

"The trials of man are of two kinds. (a) The consequences of his own actions. If a man eats too much, he ruins his digestion; if he takes poison he becomes ill or dies. If a person gambles he will lose his money; if he drinks too much he will lose his equilibrium. All these sufferings are caused by the man himself, it is quite clear therefore that certain sorrows are the result of our own deeds.

(b) Other sufferings there are, which come upon the Faithful of God. Consider the great sorrows endured by Christ and by His apostles!

Those who suffer most, attain to the greatest perfection...Tests are benefits from God, for which we should thank Him. Grief and sorrow do not come to us by chance, they are sent to us by the Divine Mercy for our own perfecting.

While a man is happy he may forget his God; but when grief comes and sorrows overwhelm him, then will he remember his Father who is in Heaven, and who is able to deliver him from his humiliations.

Men who suffer not, attain no perfection. The plant most pruned by the gardeners is that one which, when the summer comes, will have the most beautiful blossoms and the most abundant fruit." [34]

8. WHAT IS NEEDED FOR THE NEXT WORLD?

The next world is a world of lights, love of God and perfections. 'Abdu'l-Bahá explains what is needed to prepare ourselves and how this can be gained:

> "That divine world is manifestly a world of lights; therefore, man has need of illumination here. That is a world of love; the love of God is essential. It is a world of perfections; virtues, or perfections, must be acquired. That world is vivified by the breaths of the Holy Spirit; in this world we must seek them. That is the Kingdom of everlasting life; it must be attained during this vanishing existence.
>
> By what means can man acquire these things? How shall he obtain these merciful gifts and powers? First, through the knowledge of God. Second, through the love of God. Third, through faith. Fourth, through philanthropic deeds. Fifth, through self-sacrifice. Sixth, through severance from this world. Seventh, through sanctity and holiness. Unless he acquires these forces and attains to these requirements, he will surely be deprived of the life that is eternal. But if

he possesses the knowledge of God, becomes ignited through the fire of the love of God, witnesses the great and mighty signs of the Kingdom, becomes the cause of love among mankind and lives in the utmost state of sanctity and holiness, he shall surely attain to second birth, be baptized by the Holy Spirit and enjoy everlasting existence." [35]

"Our greatest efforts must be directed towards detachment from the things of the world; we must strive to become more spiritual, more luminous, to follow the counsel of the Divine Teaching, to serve the cause of unity and true equality, to be merciful, to reflect the love of the Highest on all men, so that the light of the Spirit shall be apparent in all our deeds, to the end that all humanity shall be united, the stormy sea thereof calmed, and all rough waves disappear from off the surface of life's ocean henceforth unruffled and peaceful. Then will the New Jerusalem be seen by mankind, who will enter through its gates and receive the Divine Bounty." [36]

Prayer

Prayer is essential for us to develop spiritually. It is food for our soul and we must feed our soul daily even as we feed our body. Through prayer we can also gain assistance from the next world. It is an essential part of acquiring spiritual qualities.

"Shouldst thou recite any of the revealed prayers, and seek assistance from God with thy face turned towards Him, and implore Him with devotion and fervour, thy need will be answered." [37]

Shoghi Effendi (designated Head of the Faith by 'Abdu'l-Bahá) clarifies, in answer to a question:

> "We cannot know God directly, but only through His Prophets. We can pray to Him
> realizing that through His Prophets we know Him, or we can address our prayer in
> thought to Bahá'u'lláh, not as God, but as the Door to our knowing God." [38]

The following verse from Bahá'u'lláh gives an idea of the great power of prayer:

> "Intone, O My servant, the verses of God that have been received by thee, as intoned by them who have drawn nigh unto Him, that the sweetness of thy melody may kindle thine own soul, and attract the hearts of all men. Whoso reciteth, in the privacy of his chamber, the verses revealed by God, the scattering angels of the Almighty shall scatter abroad the fragrance of the words uttered by his mouth, and shall cause the heart of every righteous man to throb. Though he may, at first, remain unaware of its effect, yet the virtue of the grace vouchsafed unto him must needs sooner or later exercise its influence upon his soul. Thus have the mysteries of the Revelation of God been decreed by virtue of the Will of Him Who is the Source of power and wisdom." [39]

9. OUR SPIRITUAL DESTINATION

Bahá'u'lláh has written about the stages of spiritual development, for example, in "The Seven Valleys".

The Tablet of Bahá'u'lláh known as "The Seven Valleys" was written using language and symbols from Sufi literature. In it is described the journey of the soul through seven valleys as it progresses spiritually. Bahá'u'lláh introduces it with this verse:

> "An exposition of the mysteries enshrined in the stages of ascent for them that seek to journey unto God, the Almighty, the Ever-Forgiving." [40]

It begins with the Valley of Search where the soul is beginning its quest. The journey continues with The Valley of Love, the Realm of Knowledge, the First Station of Unity, the City of Contentment. The sixth is the Valley of Wonderment.

The seventh valley is the Valley of True Poverty and Absolute Nothingness. Of this station Bahá'u'lláh says:

> "This is the station wherein the multiplicity of all things perisheth in the wayfarer; and the divine Countenance, dawning above the horizon of eternity, riseth out of the darkness; and the meaning of "All on

the earth shall pass away, but the face of thy Lord" is made manifest." [40]

But let us also note this exhortation of Bahá'u'lláh to mankind to listen to the "Call of God" and respond:

"The Dayspring of Glory hath, in this Day, manifested its radiance, and the Voice of the Most High is calling. We have formerly uttered these words: "This is not the day for any man to question his Lord. It behooveth whosoever hath hearkened to the Call of God, as voiced by Him Who is the Dayspring of Glory, to arise and cry out: 'Here am I, here am I, O Lord of all Names; here am I, here am I, O Maker of the heavens! I testify that, through Thy Revelation, the things hidden in the Books of God have been revealed, and that whatsoever hath been recorded by Thy Messengers in the sacred Scriptures hath been fulfilled.'" [41]

Sickness

This distinction between the soul and the body means that illness affects the body but not the soul. Bahá'u'lláh uses the analogy of the body as the mirror and the soul as the lamp reflecting in it:

"Know thou that the soul of man is exalted above, and is independent of all infirmities of body or mind. That a sick person showeth signs of weakness is due to the hindrances that interpose themselves between his soul and his body, for the soul itself remaineth unaffected by any bodily ailments. Consider the light of the lamp. Though an external object may interfere with its radiance, the light itself continueth to shine with undiminished power. In like manner, every malady afflicting the body of man is an impediment that preventeth the soul from manifesting its inherent might and power." [42]

And 'Abdu'l-Bahá explains in more detail:

"We have already explained that the spirit of man is not contained within the body, for it is freed and sanctified from egress and regress, which are among the properties of material bodies. Rather, the connection of the spirit with the body is like that of the sun with the mirror. Briefly, the human spirit is always in one condition. It neither falls ill with the illness of the body nor is made healthy by the latter's health; it does not become weak or incapacitated, wretched or downtrodden, diminished or lessened— that is, it suffers no harm or ill effect on account of the infirmities of the body, even if the body were to waste away, or if the hands, feet, and tongue were to be cut off, or if the powers of sight and hearing were to be disrupted. It is therefore evident and established that the spirit is different from the body and that its immortality is not conditioned upon the latter's, but that the spirit rules supreme in the world of the body, and that its power and influence are as plain and visible as the bounty of the sun in a mirror. But when the mirror is covered with dust or broken, it will be deprived of the rays of the sun." [43]

The Bahá'í Writings include considerable guidance on health issues and there are many prayers for healing.

Drugs – a danger to our soul

Addictive and mind-altering drugs are a serious obstacle to

spiritual progress. Bahá'u'lláh strongly condemned opium, which at that time was a grave problem. The same warning applies to similar substances. He wrote:

> "Gambling and the use of opium have been forbidden unto you. Eschew them both, O people, and be not of those who transgress. Beware of using any substance that induceth sluggishness and torpor in the human temple and inflicteth harm upon the body. We, verily, desire for you naught save what shall profit you, and to this bear witness all created things, had ye but ears to hear." [44]

And 'Abdu'l-Bahá reiterates the warning:

> "Alcohol consumeth the mind and causeth man to commit acts of absurdity, but this opium, this foul fruit of the infernal tree, and this wicked hashish extinguish the mind, freeze the spirit, petrify the soul, waste the body and leave man frustrated and lost." [45]

We should take this advice seriously as Bahá'u'lláh knows the consequences of such drugs both for our body and our soul, in this world and the next. Science has no way to monitor the soul.
Drugs give no shortcut to spiritual progress!

We now at the event we call 'death', our transition to the next world.

10. DEATH

Bahá'u'lláh made it clear to His followers that death is nothing to fear:

> "O SON OF THE SUPREME!
> I have made death a messenger of joy to thee. Wherefore dost thou grieve? I made the light to shed on thee its splendor. Why dost thou veil thyself therefrom?" [46]

He uses the analogy of the child in the womb. We leave this material world with our death and are 'born', in a sense, into the next:

> "The world beyond is as different from this world as this world is different from that of the child while still in the womb of its mother." [47]

And 'Abdu'l-Bahá comments:

> "It is similar to the condition of a human being in the womb, where his eyes are veiled, and all things are hidden away from him. Once he is born out of the uterine world and entereth this life, he findeth it, with relation to that of the womb, to be a place of perceptions and discoveries, and he observeth all things through his outer eye. In the same way, once he hath departed this life, he will behold in that world whatsoever was hidden from him here..." [48]

Another analogy used in the Writings by 'Abdu'l-Bahá is that of a bird (the soul) trapped in a cage (the body):

> "To hold that the spirit is annihilated upon the death of the body is to imagine that a bird imprisoned in a cage would perish if the cage were to be broken, though the bird has nothing to fear from the breaking of the cage. This body is even as the cage and the spirit is like the bird: We observe that this bird, unencumbered by its cage, soars freely in the world of sleep. Therefore, should the cage be broken, the bird would not only continue to exist but its senses would be heightened, its perception would be expanded, and its joy would grow more intense. In reality, it would be leaving a place of torment for a delightsome paradise; for there is no greater paradise for the grateful birds than to be freed from their cage." [49]

And yet we must expect to be held to account for our deeds:

> "Ye will most certainly be called upon to answer for His trust on the day when the Balance of Justice shall be set, the day when unto every one shall be rendered his due, when the doings of all men, be they rich or poor, shall be weighed." [50]

> "Ye, and all ye possess, shall pass away. Ye shall, most certainly, return to God, and shall be called to account for your doings in the presence of Him Who shall gather together the entire creation..." [51]

And yet Shoghi Effendi reminds us:

> "But we must always remember that our existence and everything we have or ever will have is dependent

upon the mercy of God and His bounty, and therefore He can accept into His heaven, which is really nearness to Him, even the lowliest if He pleases. We always have the hope of receiving His mercy if we reach out for it." [52]

We have looked at how we can progress in this world, but how we can progress spiritually in the next world?

11. PROGRESS IN THE NEXT WORLD

Although conditions are different, spiritual progress continues in the next world, drawing ever closer to God. For those souls who have turned towards God the next world will be joyful and happy. Moreover the next world is not just a single destination but there are "worlds, holy and spiritually glorious".

Bahá'u'lláh tells us this of the next world:

> "The Prophets and Messengers of God have been sent down for the sole purpose of guiding mankind to the straight Path of Truth. The purpose underlying Their revelation hath been to educate all men, that they may, at the hour of death, ascend, in the utmost purity and sanctity and with absolute detachment, to the throne of the Most High." [53]

> "Know thou of a truth that the soul, after its separation from the body, will continue to progress until it attaineth the presence of God, in a state and condition which neither the revolution of ages and centuries, nor the changes and chances of this world, can alter. It will endure as long as the Kingdom of God, His sovereignty, His dominion and power will endure. It will manifest the signs of God and His attributes, and will reveal His

loving kindness and bounty." [54]

"O My servants! Sorrow not if, in these days and on this earthly plane, things contrary to your wishes have been ordained and manifested by God, for days of blissful joy, of heavenly delight, are assuredly in store for you. Worlds, holy and spiritually glorious, will be unveiled to your eyes. You are destined by Him, in this world and hereafter, to partake of their benefits, to share in their joys, and to obtain a portion of their sustaining grace. To each and every one of them you will, no doubt, attain." [55]

Shoghi Effendi answered questions as follows:

"With regard to the soul of man. According to the Bahá'í Teachings the human soul starts with the formation of the human embryo, and continues to develop and pass through endless stages of existence after its separation from the body. Its progress is thus infinite." [56]

"Concerning the future life, what Bahá'u'lláh says is that the soul will continue to ascend through many worlds. What those worlds are and what their nature is we cannot know. The same way that the child in the matrix cannot know this world so we cannot know what the other world is going to be." [57]

But we do well to heed what Bahá'u'lláh wrote about our attitude to spiritual attainment:

"Humility exalteth man to the heaven of glory and power, whilst pride abaseth him to the depths of wretchedness and degradation." [58]

In this world our development can be upwards towards greater spiritual qualities or a downwards slide into a state dominated by our lower nature. 'Abdu'l-Bahá explained:

> "Man has the power both to do good and to do evil; if his power for good predominates and his inclinations to do wrong are conquered, then man in truth may be called a saint. But if, on the contrary, he rejects the things of God and allows his evil passions to conquer him, then he is no better than a mere animal." [59]

Unlike this world, in the next world progress can only be upwards:

> "...with the human soul, there is no decline. Its only movement is towards perfection; growth and progress alone constitute the motion of the soul.

> "Divine perfection is infinite, therefore the progress of the soul is also infinite. From the very birth of a human being the soul progresses, the intellect grows and knowledge increases. When the body dies the soul lives on. All the differing degrees of created physical beings are limited, but the soul is limitless!
>
> ...
>
> In the world of spirit there is no retrogression. The world of mortality is a world of contradictions, of opposites; motion being compulsory everything must either go forward or retreat. In the realm of spirit there is no retreat possible, all movement is bound to be towards a perfect state. "Progress" is the expression of spirit in the world of matter. The intelligence of man, his reasoning powers, his knowledge, his scientific achievements, all these being manifestations

of the spirit, partake of the inevitable law of spiritual progress and are, therefore, of necessity, immortal." [60]

And when we die we enter the next world with whatever spiritual qualities we have developed in this world. 'Abdu'l-Bahá again explains:

> "As to the soul of man after death, it remains in the degree of purity to which it has evolved during life in the physical body, and after it is freed from the body it remains plunged in the ocean of God's Mercy.
> From the moment the soul leaves the body and arrives in the Heavenly World, its evolution is spiritual, and that evolution is: The approaching unto God." [61]

In this world we can make spiritual progress in various ways such as through tests and trials, good deeds, prayer and so on. In the next world we are dependent on the "grace and bounty of the Lord", prayers and deeds done in our name:

> "The progress of the human spirit in the divine world, after its connection with the physical body has been severed, is either purely through the grace and bounty of the Lord, or through the intercession and prayers of other human souls, or through the significant contributions and charitable deeds which are offered in its name." [62]

"As to the second question: the tests and trials of God take place in this world, not in the world of the Kingdom." [63]

12. SERVING IN THE NEXT WORLD

Those who have developed spiritually and recognised the Manifestation of God for the age in which they live have a high station in the next world. From the next world they help advance the progress of mankind. Apparently in the next world we will not be just relaxing, there will be plenty to do.

"Just as the conception of faith hath existed from the beginning that hath no beginning, and will endure till the end that hath no end, in like manner will the true believer eternally live and endure. His spirit will everlastingly circle round the Will of God. He will last as long as God, Himself, will last. He is revealed through the Revelation of God, and is hidden at His bidding. It is evident that the loftiest mansions in the Realm of Immortality have been ordained as the habitation of them that have truly believed in God and in His signs. Death can never invade that holy seat. " [64]

"Blessed is the soul which, at the hour of its separation from the body, is sanctified from the vain imaginings of the peoples of the world. Such a soul liveth and moveth in accordance with the Will of its Creator, and entereth the all-highest Paradise. The Maids of Heaven, inmates of the loftiest mansions, will circle around it, and the Prophets of God and His chosen ones will seek its companionship. With them that soul will freely converse, and will recount unto them that which it hath been made to endure in the path of God, the Lord of all worlds. If any man be told that which hath been ordained for such a soul in the worlds of God, the Lord of the throne on high and of earth below, his whole being will instantly blaze out in his great longing to attain that most exalted, that sanctified and resplendent station..." [65]

"Thou hast, moreover, asked Me concerning the state of the soul after its separation from the body. Know thou, of a truth, that if the soul of man hath walked in the ways of God, it will, assuredly, return and be gathered to the glory of the Beloved. By the righteousness of God! It shall attain a station such as no pen can depict, or tongue describe. The soul that hath remained faithful to the Cause of God, and stood unwaveringly firm in His Path shall, after his ascension, be possessed of such power that all the worlds which the Almighty hath created can benefit through him. Such a soul provideth, at the bidding of the Ideal King and Divine Educator, the pure leaven that leaveneth the world of being, and furnisheth the power through which the arts and wonders of the world are made manifest. Consider how meal needeth leaven to be leavened with. Those souls that are the symbols of detachment are the leaven of the world. Meditate on this, and be of the thankful." [66]

"O SON OF MAN!
My eternity is My creation, I have created it for thee.

Make it the garment of thy temple. My unity is My handiwork; I have wrought it for thee; clothe thyself therewith, that thou mayest be to all eternity the revelation of My everlasting being." [67]

13. SOME ASPECTS OF THE NEXT WORLD

We cannot understand that of which we have had no similar experience. We have no physical form in the next world, no physical characteristics such as age, colour, race, gender or size. Bahá'u'lláh wrote about the nature of that world and some further comments come from 'Abdu'l-Bahá and Shoghi Effendi:

> "The nature of the soul after death can never be described, nor is it meet and permissible to reveal its whole character to the eyes of men." [68]

> "The world beyond is as different from this world as this world is different from that of the child while still in the womb of its mother. When the soul attaineth the Presence of God, it will assume the form that best befitteth its immortality and is worthy of its celestial habitation." [69]

> "The answer to the third question is this, that in the other world the human reality doth not assume a physical form, rather doth it take on a heavenly form, made up of elements of that heavenly realm.

And the answer to the fourth question: The centre of the Sun of Truth is in the supernal world–the Kingdom of God. Those souls who are pure and unsullied, upon the dissolution of their elemental frames, hasten away to the world of God, and that world is within this world. The people of this world, however, are unaware of that world, and are even as the mineral and the vegetable that know nothing of the world of the animal and the world of man." [70]

"The Guardian feels that, while there is no harm in speculation on these abstract matters, one should not attach too much importance to them. Science itself is far from having resolved the question of the nature of matter, and we cannot, in this physical world, grasp the spiritual one more than in a very fragmentary and inadequate manner." [71]

In the next world we will be able to meet other souls we have known and other great souls, but differences in spiritual attributes becomes important:

"As to thy question regarding discoveries made by the soul after it hath put off its human form: certainly, that world is a world of perceptions and discoveries, for the interposed veil will be lifted away and the human spirit will gaze upon souls that are above, below, and on a par with itself. It is similar to the condition of a human being in the womb, where his eyes are veiled, and all things are hidden away from him. Once he is born out of the uterine world and entereth this life, he findeth it, with relation to that of the womb, to be a place of perceptions and discoveries, and he observeth all things through his outer eye. In the same way, once he hath departed this life, he will behold in that world whatsoever was hidden from him here: but there he will look upon and comprehend all things with his inner eye. There will he gaze on his fellows and his peers, and those in the ranks above him, and those below. As for what is meant by the equality of souls in the all-highest realm, it is this: the souls of the believers, at the time when they first become manifest in the world of the body, are equal, and each is sanctified and pure. In this world, however, they will begin to differ one from another, some achieving the highest station, some a middle one, others remaining at the lowest stage of being. Their equal status is at the beginning of their existence; the differentiation followeth their passing away." [72]

Prayer in the next world

Prayer has power whether we are in this world or in the next. 'Abdu'l-Bahá was reported to say "In prayer there is a mingling of station, a mingling of condition. Pray for them as they pray for you!" [73]

Mention has already been made above of prayers regarding intercession where souls ask for help for others. We repeat part of that quotation here:

> "The progress of the human spirit in the divine world, after its connection with the physical body has been severed, is either purely through the grace and bounty of the Lord, or through the intercession and prayers of other human souls..." [74]

The prayers given to us by Bahá'u'lláh have special power because they are the Word of God. There are many, many prayers including those for the departed, for healing, forgiveness, spirituality, women, children and so on. There is special prayer for the dead which is read only at Bahá'í funerals.

As above, so below

For centuries some have observed that spiritual laws and laws of the material world tend to parallel each other. 'Abdu'l-Bahá confirms this as follows:

> "The spiritual world is like unto the phenomenal world. They are the exact counterpart of each other. Whatever objects appear in this world of existence are the outer pictures of the world of heaven." [75]

He goes on to describe how the pattern of progressive revelation and the rise and decline of religions is analogous to the seasons of spring, summer, autumn and winter. There are many more examples.

It seems that it is God's intention for us to learn of things in this world which will then help us understand spiritual laws and how things work in the next world.

> "Every created thing in the whole universe is but a door leading into His knowledge, a sign of His sovereignty, a revelation of His names, a symbol of His majesty, a token of His power, a means of admittance into His straight Path...." [76]

14. ANGELS

While we cannot really understand the next world and those beings who live in it, the Writings do give us some insights. We do not attempt to go deep into this complex topic.

First, regarding angels, according to Bahá'í teachings, angels are not only found in the next world. Bahá'u'lláh Himself explains:

> "And now, concerning His words: "And He shall send His angels...." By "angels" is meant those who, reinforced by the power of the spirit, have consumed, with the fire of the love of God, all human traits and limitations, and have clothed themselves with the attributes of the most exalted Beings and of the Cherubim." [77]

> "And now, inasmuch as these holy beings have sanctified themselves from every human limitation, have become endowed with the attributes of the spiritual, and have been adorned with the noble traits of the blessed, they therefore have been designated as "angels." " [78]

(Note: The writer has not found a clear explanation of the meaning of 'Cherubim' in this context.)
'Abdu'l-Bahá has said:

"Ye are the angels, if your feet be firm, your spirits rejoiced, your secret thoughts pure, your eyes consoled, your ears opened, your breasts dilated with joy, and your souls gladdened, and if you arise to assist the Covenant, to resist dissension and to be attracted to the Effulgence!" [79]

Then there is the term 'concourse'. It is used as a collective word for the followers of Bahá'u'lláh while the term 'Concourse on High' seems to be used at times to refer to those in the next world.

"Verily, We behold you from Our realm of glory, and shall aid whosoever will arise for the triumph of Our Cause with the hosts of the Concourse on high and a company of Our favored angels." [80]

And then there is the 'Supreme Concourse':

"By My life and My Cause! Round about whatever dwelling the friends of God may enter, and from which their cry shall rise as they praise and glorify the Lord, shall circle the souls of true believers and all the favoured angels. And should the door of the true eye be opened unto some, they shall witness the Supreme Concourse as it circleth and crieth: Blessed art thou, O house,..." [81]

In other passages various other terms are used.

15.
MISCONCEPTIONS AND MISCELLANEOUS TOPICS

Now we will look at a few other related topics such as losses and disasters, the question of evil, some background on Bahá'í holy places and reincarnation.

Consolation on the loss of a loved one

'Abdu'l-Bahá offers consolation to a mother who has lost a son, asking her not to "wail nor weep; for agitation and mourning deeply affect his soul" and assuring her that they will meet again:

> "O thou beloved maidservant of God, although the loss of a son is indeed heartbreaking and beyond the limits of human endurance, yet one who knoweth and understandeth is assured that the son hath not been lost but, rather, hath stepped from this world into another, and she will find him in the divine realm.

That reunion shall be for eternity, while in this world separation is inevitable and bringeth with it a burning grief.

Praise be unto God that thou hast faith, art turning thy face toward the everlasting Kingdom and believest in the existence of a heavenly world. Therefore be thou not disconsolate, do not languish, do not sigh, neither wail nor weep; for agitation and mourning deeply affect his soul in the divine realm.

That beloved child addresseth thee from the hidden world: "O thou kind Mother, thank divine Providence that I have been freed from a small and gloomy cage and, like the birds of the meadows, have soared to the divine world—a world which is spacious, illumined, and ever gay and jubilant. Therefore, lament not, O Mother, and be not grieved; I am not of the lost, nor have I been obliterated and destroyed. I have shaken off the mortal form and have raised my banner in this spiritual world. Following this separation is everlasting companionship. Thou shalt find me in the heaven of the Lord, immersed in an ocean of light." [82]

Disasters and loss of life

When 'Abdu'l-Bahá was traveling to the United States in 1912 He chose not to travel on the Titanic but on an older ship. After the disastrous sinking of the Titanic He talked about such disasters and the spiritual perspective:

"Within the last few days a terrible event has happened in the world, an event saddening to every heart and grieving every spirit. I refer to the Titanic disaster, in which many of our fellow human beings were drowned, a number of beautiful souls passed beyond this earthly life. Although such an event is indeed regrettable, we must realize that everything which happens is due to some wisdom and that nothing happens without a reason. Therein is a mystery; but whatever the reason and mystery, it was a very sad occurrence, one which brought tears to many eyes and distress to many souls. I was greatly affected by this disaster. Some of those who were lost voyaged on the Cedric with us as far as Naples and afterward sailed upon the other ship. When I think of them, I am very sad indeed. But when I consider this calamity in another aspect, I am consoled by the realization that the worlds of God are infinite; that though they were deprived of this existence, they have other opportunities in the life beyond, even as Christ has said, "In my Father's house are many mansions." They were called away from the temporary and transferred to the eternal; they abandoned this material existence and entered the portals of the spiritual world. Foregoing the pleasures and comforts of the earthly, they now partake of a joy and happiness far more abiding and real, for they have hastened to the Kingdom of God. The mercy of God is infinite, and it is our duty to remember these departed souls in our prayers and supplications that they may draw nearer and nearer to the Source itself." [83]

Evil

This subject has perplexed man for ages and has led to many strange beliefs and practices. According to Bahá'í teachings evil has no real existence but is the absence of good.

Here is 'Abdu'l-Bahá's explanation on this question:

"To explain the truth of this matter is difficult indeed. Know that created things are of two kinds: material and spiritual, sensible and intelligible. That is, some are perceptible to the senses, while others are only perceived by the mind.

Sensible realities are those which are perceived by the five outer senses: So, for example, those outward things which the eye sees are called sensible. Intelligible realities are those which have no outward existence but are perceived by the mind. For example, the mind itself is an intelligible reality and has no outward existence. Likewise, all human virtues and attributes have an intelligible rather than a sensible existence; that is, they are realities that are perceived by the mind and not by the senses.

Briefly, intelligible realities such as the praiseworthy attributes and perfections of man are purely good and have a positive existence. Evil is simply their non-existence. So ignorance is the want of knowledge, error is the want of guidance, forgetfulness is the want of remembrance, foolishness is the want of understanding: All these are nothing in themselves and have no positive existence.

As for sensible realities, these are also purely good, and evil is merely their non-existence; that is, blindness is the want of sight, deafness is the want of hearing, poverty is the want of wealth, illness is the want of health, death is the want of life, and weakness is the want of strength.

Now, a doubt comes to mind: Scorpions and snakes are poisonous—is this good or evil, for they have a positive existence? Yes, it is true that scorpions and snakes are evil, but only in relation to us and not to themselves, for their venom is their weapon and their sting their means of defence. But as the constituent elements of their venom are incompatible with those of our bodies —that is, as these constituent elements are mutually opposed—the venom is evil, or rather, those elements are evil in relation to each other, while in their own reality they are both good.

To summarize, one thing may be evil in relation to another but not evil within the limits of its own being. It follows therefore that there is no evil in existence: Whatsoever God has created, He has created good. Evil consists merely in non-existence. For example, death is the absence of life: When man is no longer sustained by the power of life, he dies. Darkness is the absence of light: When light is no more, darkness reigns. Light is a positively existing thing, but darkness has no positive existence; it is merely its absence. Likewise, wealth is a positively existing thing but poverty is merely its absence.

It is thus evident that all evil is mere non-existence. Good has a positive existence; evil is merely its absence." [84]

Hell

Given the above explanation of evil it follows that the popular conception of hell and its inhabitants are likewise non-existent.

The reference to hell in scriptures is symbolic of the fate of those who leave this world without spiritual qualities. They find themselves with others of their kind, unable to fully participate in the spiritual worlds, dependent on the mercy of God.

Evil souls

'Abdu'l-Bahá was asked about 'earth-bound souls' and 'evil souls':

> "There are no earth-bound souls. When the souls that are not good die they go entirely away from this earth and so cannot influence anyone. They are spiritually dead. Their thoughts can have influence only when they are alive on the earth...
> But the good souls are given eternal life and sometimes God permits their thoughts to reach the earth to help the people." [85]

> "There is no power exercised over the people by those evil souls that have passed away. Good is stronger than evil and even when alive they had very little power. How much less have they after they are dead, and besides they are nowhere near this planet." [86]

Psychic forces

'Abdu'l-Bahá does not deny the existence of psychic forces (telepathy etc) but states that it is unwise to encourage the use of such things as they belong to the next world, not this:

> "To tamper with psychic forces while in this world interferes with the condition of the soul in the world

to come. These forces are real, but, normally, are not active on this plane. The child in the womb has its eyes, ears, hands, feet, etc., but they are not in activity. The whole purpose of life in the material world is the coming forth into the world of Reality, where those forces will become active. They belong to that world." [87]

Holy places

There are many holy places associated with the Faith. These include the shrines of the three central figures of the Faith, Bahá'u'lláh, the Báb and 'Abdu'l-Bahá which are all located in Israel. They have been there for more than one hundred years. There are also places of pilgrimage and many graves of 'martyrs and holy souls' scattered around the world.

'Abdu'l-Bahá stated:

"You have asked about visiting holy places and the observance of marked reverence toward these resplendent spots. Holy places are undoubtedly centres of the outpouring of Divine grace, because on entering the illumined sites associated with martyrs and holy souls, and by observing reverence, both physical and spiritual, one's heart is moved with great tenderness. But there is no obligation for everyone to visit such places, other than the three, namely... (see note below). But as to the other resting places of martyrs and holy souls, it is pleasing and acceptable in the sight of God if a person desires to draw nigh unto Him by visiting them; this, however, is not a binding obligation." [88]

Note: the three places named are the 'Most Holy Shrine' (of

Bahá'u'lláh), the 'Blessed House in Baghdad' (the House of Bahá'u'lláh) and the 'venerated House of The Báb' in Shiraz. At present only the first is open for pilgrimage. The third was destroyed by Iranian authorities some years ago as part of their on-going persecution of the Faith.

In many cases there are special prayers (Tablets of Visitation) revealed for use when visiting these sites.

Burial

It seems appropriate to make a brief mention of this topic. Burial according to Bahá'í teachings is quite simple and dignified but several rules do apply. Burial (not cremation) should take place at a site within one hour's journey. The Prayer for the Dead should be read by one person. Other prayers can also be said.

Reincarnation

'Abdu'l-Bahá gives a detailed explanation of this subject in Some Answered Questions[89] but Shoghi Effendi made this brief summary:

"The Bahá'í view of reincarnation is essentially different from the Hindu conception. The Bahá'ís believe in the return of the attributes and qualities, but maintain that the essence or the reality of things cannot be made to return. Every being keeps its own individuality, but some of his qualities can be transmitted. The doctrine of metempsychosis upheld by the Hindus is fallacious." [90]

Our souls do not return to this material world.

We conclude this part with a selection of Bahá'í prayers for the departed.

16. SOME PRAYERS FOR THE DEPARTED

It is interesting to note that prayers such as these often contain hints of the world to come e.g. "the garden of happiness", "Thine exalted rose garden", "the sea of light in the world of mysteries" and so on.

"Glory be to Thee, O Lord my God! Abase not him whom Thou hast exalted through the power of Thine everlasting sovereignty, and remove not far from Thee him whom Thou hast caused to enter the tabernacle of Thine eternity. Wilt Thou cast away, O my God, him whom Thou hast overshadowed with Thy Lordship, and wilt Thou turn away from Thee, O my Desire, him to whom Thou hast been a refuge? Canst Thou degrade him whom Thou hast uplifted, or forget him whom Thou didst enable to remember Thee?

Glorified, immensely glorified art Thou! Thou art He Who from everlasting hath been the King of the entire creation and its Prime Mover, and Thou wilt to everlasting remain the Lord of all created things and their Ordainer. Glorified art Thou, O my God! If Thou ceasest to be merciful unto Thy servants, who, then, will show mercy unto them; and if Thou refusest to succor Thy loved ones, who is there that can succor them?

Glorified, immeasurably glorified art Thou! Thou art adored in Thy truth, and Thee do we all, verily, worship; and Thou art manifest in Thy justice, and to Thee do we all, verily, bear witness. Thou art, in truth, beloved in Thy grace. No God is there but Thee, the Help in Peril, the Self-Subsisting." [91]
—Bahá'u'lláh

***

"O my God! O Thou forgiver of sins, bestower of gifts, dispeller of afflictions!

Verily, I beseech Thee to forgive the sins of such as have abandoned the physical garment and have ascended to the spiritual world.

O my Lord! Purify them from trespasses, dispel their sorrows, and change their darkness into light. Cause them to enter the garden of happiness, cleanse them with the most pure water, and grant them to behold Thy splendors on the loftiest mount." [92]
— 'Abdu'l-Bahá

***

"O my God! O my God! Verily, Thy servant, humble before the majesty of Thy divine supremacy, lowly at the door of Thy oneness, hath believed in Thee and in Thy verses, hath testified to Thy word, hath been enkindled with the fire of Thy love, hath been immersed in the depths of the ocean of Thy knowledge, hath been attracted by Thy breezes, hath relied upon Thee, hath turned his face to Thee, hath offered his supplications to Thee, and hath been assured of Thy pardon and forgiveness. He hath abandoned this mortal life and hath flown to the kingdom of immortality, yearning for the favor of meeting Thee. O Lord, glorify his station, shelter him under the pavilion of Thy supreme mercy, cause him to enter Thy glorious paradise, and perpetuate his existence in Thine exalted rose garden, that he may plunge into the sea of light in the world of mysteries.Verily, Thou art the Generous, the Powerful, the Forgiver and the Bestower." [93]

— 'Abdu'l-Bahá

***

"O Thou forgiving Lord!

Although some souls have spent the days of their lives in ignorance, and became estranged and contumacious, yet, with one wave from the ocean of Thy forgiveness, all those encompassed by sin will be set free. Whomsoever Thou willest Thou makest a confidant, and whosoever is not the object of Thy choice is accounted a transgressor. Shouldst Thou deal with us with Thy justice, we are all naught but sinners and deserving to be shut out from Thee, but shouldst Thou uphold mercy, every sinner would be made pure and every stranger a friend. Bestow, then, Thy forgiveness and pardon, and grant Thy mercy unto all.

Thou art the Forgiver, the Lightgiver and the Omnipotent." [94]

— 'Abdu'l-Bahá

FOR WOMEN

"O my God, O Forgiver of sins and Dispeller of

afflictions! O Thou Who art the Pardoner, the Merciful! I raise my suppliant hands to Thee, tearfully beseeching the court of Thy divine Essence to forgive, through Thy grace and clemency, Thy handmaiden who hath ascended unto the seat of truth. Cause her, O Lord, to be overshadowed by the clouds of Thy bounty and favor, immerse her in the ocean of Thy forgiveness and pardon, and enable her to enter that sanctified abode, Thy heavenly Paradise.

Thou art, verily, the Mighty, the Compassionate, the Generous, the Merciful." [95]
— 'Abdu'l-Bahá

***

"O Lord, O Thou Whose mercy hath encompassed all, Whose forgiveness is transcendent, Whose bounty is sublime, Whose pardon and generosity are all-embracing, and the lights of Whose forgiveness are diffused throughout the world! O Lord of glory! I entreat Thee, fervently and tearfully, to cast upon Thy handmaiden who hath ascended unto Thee the glances of the eye of Thy mercy. Robe her in the mantle of Thy grace, bright with the ornaments of the celestial Paradise, and, sheltering her beneath the tree of Thy oneness, illumine her face with the lights of Thy mercy and compassion.

Bestow upon Thy heavenly handmaiden, O God, the holy fragrances born of the spirit of Thy forgiveness. Cause her to dwell in a blissful abode, heal her griefs with the balm of Thy reunion, and, in accordance with Thy will, grant her admission to Thy holy Paradise. Let the angels of Thy loving-kindness descend successively upon her, and shelter her beneath Thy blessed Tree. Thou art, verily, the Ever-Forgiving, the Most Generous, the All-Bountiful." [96]

— 'Abdu'l-Bahá

APPENDIX A - AN OVERVIEW OF THE BAHÁ'Í FAITH

Some teachings for this new age

The central teaching of the Bahá'í Faith is that mankind is one people and that this planet is the home of all of us. This becomes more evident with every year. More and more problems arise which require global cooperation to solve. Delaying acceptance of this principle only increases our troubles. This acceptance is an aspect of humanity's growing maturity. Bahá'u'lláh wrote:

> "O contending peoples and kindreds of the earth! Set your faces towards unity, and let the radiance of its light shine upon you. Gather ye together, and for the sake of God resolve to root out whatever is the source of contention amongst you. ... There can be no doubt whatever that the peoples of the world, of whatever race or religion, derive their inspiration from one heavenly Source, and are the subjects of one God." [98]

Science also indicates that all of mankind has one origin. And that there is only one race – the human race. The differences between us provide an interesting and dynamic diversity. Unity in diversity.

Mankind has been compared with a flower garden composed of flowers of many colours.

Bahá'u'lláh said that He had been sent by God to bring about this unity of the peoples of the world. He compared Himself with a physician sent to a sick patient with the remedy needed for his sickness. The remedy is not the same as that needed in previous times.

While in prison Bahá'u'lláh wrote to the kings and rulers of the day informing them of His mission. He called on them to care for their people, to be just and to establish peace between nations. He warned them of dire consequences for mankind if they did not take heed.

His Writings fill many volumes and cover many subjects ranging from the nature of the soul and life after death to society and economics. He has given clear guidance on how to build a new society free of the problems that trouble us today.

Some of the main teachings can be listed as follows:

1. Abandonment of all forms of prejudice
2. Equality of opportunity of women and men
3. Unity of religion
4. Elimination of extremes of poverty and wealth
5. Universal education
6. Independent search for truth

7. Establishment of a global commonwealth of nations
8. True religion is in harmony with science

How the Bahá'í Faith began

The Faith began in 1844 in Shiraz, Iran. During those days many were expecting the fulfillment of prophecies from the Bible and the Qur'an.

A young student who was searching for the One foretold by prophecy was met at the gate of the city of Shiraz by a young merchant and invited to His home. This merchant, Whom we know of as the Báb (meaning "Gate"), declared to this seeker that He was the Promised One, sent by God with teachings for the new age. A new Revelation began. Many more seekers soon found and recognised Him independently of each other.

His teachings such as new laws, the abolition of the clergy and the equality of rights of men and women caused an uproar in Iran among the Muslim clergy and the rulers. During the few years remaining in His mission, the Báb prepared His followers for the coming of a greater

Revelation soon to appear.

Thousands of the followers of the Báb gave their lives for the new Faith and the Báb Himself was imprisoned, tortured and finally executed in 1850. His beautiful and sacred shrine is on Mount Carmel in what is now Israel.

Who is Bahá'u'lláh?

Bahá'u'lláh (a title meaning "the Glory of God") was born in Iran in 1817. He was known for His kindness, wisdom, generosity and spirituality. And for His lack of interest in worldly power. He was the One promised by the Báb.

Bahá'u'lláh supported the Báb and was imprisoned for this reason in 1853. While in prison He was called by God to deliver teachings needed for this new age. He undertook this mission knowing it would lead to suffering and persecution. He was exiled to Baghdad, Iraq, with His family a few months later. In 1863 He publicly declared His mission to some of His followers. He succeeded in reviving the discouraged followers of the Báb. Through His inspiration and love the new Faith thrived.

The clergy were worried. They could not defeat Him in debate and the new Faith was growing. They had Him exiled again, this time to Constantinople. After many years of further imprisonment and exile but undeterred, He was sent to the prison city of Akka by the Turkish Empire. At that time Akka was in Palestine but that land is now Israel. His arrival there fulfilled many prophecies.

While in prison He wrote many letters and books and His teachings spread as far as India, Egypt and Europe. He laid the foundations for a new world order based on justice, unity and peace. He passed away in 1892, His mission accomplished.

Sacrifice, persecution and suffering has been the lot of all of God's divine Messengers but this has never stopped God's purpose from being achieved.

After the passing of Bahá'u'lláh

The history of the Faith covers some 200 years and is fascinating, rich and complex. Below is a very brief outline of this history from 1892.

Bahá'u'lláh, in His will, named His eldest son 'Abdu'l-Bahá as Head of the Faith after Him. 'Abdu'l-Bahá was also a prisoner with Bahá'u'lláh for most of His life and often represented Him.

While 'Abdu'l-Bahá did have a high spiritual station it was not that of a Manifestation like His Father. He had a unique role and Bahá'u'lláh named Him as the authorized interpreter of His teachings and the Centre of His Covenant, a role to which 'Abdu'l-Bahá was completely faithful. He was also the perfect exemplar of Bahá'u'lláh's teachings and all were called upon to turn to Him.

After the passing of Bahá'u'lláh, the Faith continued to progress especially in Asia, Europe and North America. 'Abdu'l-Bahá was finally released when He was in His late sixties and He then traveled to Egypt, Europe and North America. He spoke of peace and justice to the leaders of these countries and to people in all walks of life. He passed on in 1921.

'Abdu'l-Bahá had named His grandson, Shoghi Effendi, as Head of the Faith in His will. Under Shoghi Effendi, the

Faith continued to progress and became more structured following guidelines laid down in the Writings. The Faith reached almost every country and territory in the world. This lead eventually to the election in 1963 of the Universal House of Justice, the head governing body of the Faith as described by Bahá'u'lláh. There are no clergy.

Universal House of Justice is elected every five years. National administrative bodies are elected every year as are similar bodies at the local level. These local bodies look after community affairs including classes for children  and youth, community meetings and training programs.

A notable aspect of the history of the Faith is that while the Faith has expanded rapidly in the West, the relentless, unjustified opposition to the Faith started in the time of the Báb by the Muslim clergy in Iran has continued to this day. This has attracted the attention of the UN which has repeatedly condemned the persecution and the failed attempts to wipe out the Bahá'í community in Iran with executions, destruction of property and denial of human rights.

Today the Bahá'í Faith is recognised as an independent world religion established in almost every country and having a united, growing and diverse community.

APPENDIX B – NEAR-DEATH EXPERIENCES (NDES)

According to Wikipedia:

> "A near-death experience (NDE) is a profound personal experience associated with death or impending death which researchers claim share similar characteristics. When positive, such experiences may encompass a variety of sensations including detachment from the body, feelings of levitation, total serenity, security, warmth, the experience of absolute dissolution, and the presence of a light. When negative, such experiences may include sensations of anguish and distress." [97]

Researchers in the field report that a significant percentage (perhaps ten percent or more) of those surviving a cardiac arrest and resuscitation in the US experience an NDE. NDEs also occur under various other circumstances. The NDE experience, while personal, has common elements. These are listed by Wikipedia as follows:

"Common traits that have been reported by NDErs are as follows:

- A sense/awareness of being dead.
- A sense of peace, well-being and painlessness. Positive emotions. A sense of removal from the world.
- An out-of-body experience. A perception of one's body from an outside position, sometimes observing medical professionals performing resuscitation efforts.
- A "tunnel experience" or entering a darkness. A sense of moving up, or through, a passageway or staircase.
- A rapid movement toward and/or sudden immersion in a powerful light (or "Being of Light") which communicates telepathically with the person.
- An intense feeling of unconditional love and acceptance.
- Encountering "Beings of Light", "Beings dressed in white", or similar. Also, the possibility of being reunited with deceased loved ones.
- Receiving a life review, commonly referred to as "seeing one's life flash before one's eyes".
- Approaching a border or a decision by oneself or others to return to one's body, often accompanied by a reluctance to return.
- Suddenly finding oneself back inside one's body.
- Connection to the cultural beliefs held by the individual, which seem to dictate some of the phenomena experienced in the NDE and particularly the later interpretation thereof." [97]

There seems to be a basic agreement with Bahá'í teachings on life after death. Especially relevant are the Bahá'í teachings on the existence of God and life after death, unity of religion, and immortality of the soul. Near death experiences would likely be no surprise to most Bahá'ís.

This is a big subject and has a large body of literature and research which we cannot explore here. In recent years the International Association for Near-Death Studies has been formed for those with such experiences. There is also a constant stream of books being published giving accounts of NDEs.

More on NDEs:

International Association for Near-Death Studies
 https://www.iands.org/

"Scientific Evidence Supporting Near-Death Experiences and the Afterlife" https://near-death.com/afterlife-evidence/

Near-Death Experience Research Foundation https://www.nderf.org/

"Near-Death Studies", Wikipedia https://en.wikipedia.org/wiki/Near-death_studies

"Near-Death Experience", Wikipedia https://en.wikipedia.org/wiki/Near-death_experience

BIOGRAPHY

For further reading and online sources, see below.

'Abdu'l-Bahá in London. 'Abdu'l-Bahá. (Out of print)

Bahá'í Meetings. Compilation Prepared by the Research Department of the Universal House of Justice.

Bahá'í Prayers. Bahá'í Publishing Trust (USA).

Bahá'í World Faith. 'Abdu'l-Bahá. Bahá'í Publishing Trust. (Out of print)

Bahá'u'lláh and the New Era. J. E. Esslemont. Bahá'í Publishing (UK).

Call of the Divine Beloved, The. Bahá'u'lláh. Bahá'í Publishing (US).

Daily Lessons, Received at Akka. 'Abdu'l-Bahá.

Dawn of a New Day. Shoghi Effendi. Bahá'í Publishing Trust (India).

Gleanings from the Writings of Bahá'u'lláh. Bahá'u'lláh. Bahá'í Publishing Trust (USA).

Hidden Words. Bahá'u'lláh. Bahá'í Publishing Trust (USA).

High Endeavors: Messages to Alaska. Shoghi Effendi.

Kitáb-i-Aqdas, The. Bahá'u'lláh. Bahá'í Publishing Trust (USA).

Kitáb-i-Íqán, The. Bahá'u'lláh. Bahá'í Publishing Trust (USA).

Lights of Guidance. Compiled by Helen Bassett Hornby. Bahá'í Publishing Trust (India).

Paris Talks. 'Abdu'l-Bahá. Bahá'í Publishing Trust (UK).

Promulgation of Universal Peace, The. 'Abdu'l-Bahá. Bahá'í Publishing Trust (USA).

Selections from the Writings of 'Abdu'l-Bahá. 'Abdu'l-Bahá. Bahá'í Publishing Trust (USA).

Some Answered Questions. 'Abdu'l-Bahá. Bahá'í Publishing Trust (USA).

Synopsis and Codification of the Laws and Ordinances of the Kitáb-i-Aqdas. Shoghi Effendi. Bahá'í Publishing Trust (USA).

Tablets of Bahá'u'lláh. Bahá'u'lláh. Bahá'í Publishing Trust (USA).

REFERENCES

Note: all these texts are available on the main international website – see Links below.

The organisation of these texts varies between titles and editions. Some are referenced by section number, some by page and some by date.

1. Gleanings from the Writings of Bahá'u'lláh. Bahá'u'lláh. LXXXI p. 158
2. Paris Talks. 'Abdu'l-Bahá. 22nd November 1912.
3. 'Abdu'l-Bahá in London. 'Abdu'l-Bahá. p. 95
4. Gleanings from the Writings of Bahá'u'lláh. Bahá'u'lláh. CLIII p. 329
5. "What Psychology Says About Materialism and the Holidays". Tim Kasser. American Psychological Association. Press release December 2014.
6. "Death". Wikipedia website. https://en.wikipedia.org/wiki/Death
7. ibid.
8. NDE Prospective Study (Press release). Pim Van Lommel. NDERF website. https://www.nderf.org/NDERF/Research/NDE%20Article%20Press%20Release.htm
9. "Death isn't scary – if you've had a near-death experience". Natasha Tassell-Matamua. The Conversation website. https://theconversation.com/death-isnt-scary-if-youve-

had-a-near-death-experience-32557
10. Gleanings from the Writings of Bahá'u'lláh. Bahá'u'lláh. XIX p. 46
11. Hidden Words (Arabic). Bahá'u'lláh. 65
12. Gleanings from the Writings of Bahá'u'lláh. Bahá'u'lláh. XIX p. 47
13. ibid. XXI p. 49
14. ibid. LXXVI p. 145
15. ibid. LIV p. 108
16. Bahá'í Prayers. Bahá'u'lláh.
17. Gleanings from the Writings of Bahá'u'lláh. Bahá'u'lláh. XXXIV p. 77
18. ibid. LIX p. 115
19. Hidden Words (Arabic). Bahá'u'lláh. 1
20. Gleanings from the Writings of Bahá'u'lláh. Bahá'u'lláh. LXXXI p. 155
21. ibid. CLIII p. 323
22. Hidden Words (Arabic). Bahá'u'lláh. 55
23. Gleanings from the Writings of Bahá'u'lláh. Bahá'u'lláh. LXXXII p. 158
24. Hidden Words (Arabic). Bahá'u'lláh. 27
25. Paris Talks. 'Abdu'l-Bahá. 10th November 1912
26. Promulgation of Universal Peace, The. 'Abdu'l-Bahá. 26th August 1912. p. 283
27. Some Answered Questions. 'Abdu'l-Bahá. 66
28. Gleanings from the Writings of Bahá'u'lláh. Bahá'u'lláh. XXVII p. 65
29. Some Answered Questions. 'Abdu'l-Bahá. 55
30. Gleanings from the Writings of Bahá'u'lláh. Bahá'u'lláh. LXXVII p. 149
31. Tablets of Bahá'u'lláh. Bahá'u'lláh. 12
32. Promulgation of Universal Peace, The. 'Abdu'l-Bahá. 24th July 1912. p. 239

33. Paris Talks. 'Abdu'l-Bahá. 22nd November 1912
34. ibid. 27th October 1912
35. Promulgation of Universal Peace, The. 'Abdu'l-Bahá. 6th July 1912. p. 225
36. Paris Talks. 'Abdu'l-Bahá. 9th November 1912
37. Prayer and Devotional Life. 'Abdu'l-Bahá. Para 6
38. High Endeavors: Messages to Alaska. Shoghi Effendi. p. 71
39. Gleanings from the Writings of Bahá'u'lláh. Bahá'u'lláh. CXXXVI p. 295
40. The Seven Valleys, Call of the Divine Beloved, The. Bahá'u'lláh.
41. Gleanings from the Writings of Bahá'u'lláh. Bahá'u'lláh. LXXXII p. 158
42. ibid. LXXX p. 153
43. Some Answered Questions. 'Abdu'l-Bahá. 61
44. Kitáb-i-Aqdas, The. Bahá'u'lláh. 155
45. ibid. Note 170
46. Hidden Words (Arabic). Bahá'u'lláh. 32
47. Gleanings from the Writings of Bahá'u'lláh. Bahá'u'lláh. LXXXI p. 155
48. Selections from the Writings of 'Abdu'l-Bahá. 'Abdu'l-Bahá. 145
49. Some Answered Questions. 'Abdu'l-Bahá. 61
50. Gleanings from the Writings of Bahá'u'lláh. Bahá'u'lláh. CXVIII p. 250
51. ibid. CXVI p. 246
52. Lights of Guidance. Shoghi Effendi. 705
53. Gleanings from the Writings of Bahá'u'lláh. Bahá'u'lláh. LXXXI p. 155
54. ibid. LXXXI p. 155
55. ibid. CLIII p. 329
56. Lights of Guidance. Shoghi Effendi. 680

57. ibid. 682
58. Tablets of Bahá'u'lláh. Bahá'u'lláh. 6
59. Paris Talks. 'Abdu'l-Bahá. 3rd November 1912
60. ibid. 10th November 1912
61. ibid. 3rd November 1912
62. Some Answered Questions. 'Abdu'l-Bahá. 66
63. Selections from the Writings of 'Abdu'l-Bahá. 'Abdu'l-Bahá. 163
64. Gleanings from the Writings of Bahá'u'lláh. Bahá'u'lláh. LXXIII p. 140
65. ibid. LXXXI p. 155
66. ibid. LXXXII p. 158
67. Hidden Words (Arabic). Bahá'u'lláh. 64
68. Gleanings from the Writings of Bahá'u'lláh. Bahá'u'lláh. LXXXI p. 155
69. ibid. LXXXI p. 155
70. Selections from the Writings of 'Abdu'l-Bahá. 'Abdu'l-Bahá. 163
71. Lights of Guidance. Shoghi Effendi. 702
72. Selections from the Writings of 'Abdu'l-Bahá. 'Abdu'l-Bahá. 145
73. 'Abdu'l-Bahá in London. 'Abdu'l-Bahá. p. 96
74. Some Answered Questions. 'Abdu'l-Bahá. 66
75. Promulgation of Universal Peace, The. 'Abdu'l-Bahá. 13th April 1912. p. 10
76. Gleanings from the Writings of Bahá'u'lláh. Bahá'u'lláh. LXXXII p. 158
77. Kitáb-i-Íqán, The. Bahá'u'lláh. v86 p. 73
78. ibid. v87 p. 74
79. Bahá'í World Faith. 'Abdu'l-Bahá. p. 360
80. Gleanings from the Writings of Bahá'u'lláh. Bahá'u'lláh. LXXII p. 139
81. Bahá'í Meetings. Compilation Prepared by the

Research Department of the Universal House of Justice. 2

82. Selections from the Writings of 'Abdu'l-Bahá. 'Abdu'l-Bahá. 171

83. Promulgation of Universal Peace, The. 'Abdu'l-Bahá. 23rd April 1912. 6 p. 46

84. Some Answered Questions. 'Abdu'l-Bahá. 74

85. Daily Lessons, Received at Akka. 'Abdu'l-Bahá. p. 35

86. ibid. p. 43

87. Bahá'u'lláh and the New Era. Esslemont. p. 193

88. Synopsis and Codification of the Laws and Ordinances of the Kitáb-i-Aqdas. Shoghi Effendi. p. 61

89. Some Answered Questions. 'Abdu'l-Bahá. 81

90. Dawn of a New Day. Shoghi Effendi. p. 201

91. Bahá'í Prayers. Bahá'u'lláh.

92. Bahá'í Prayers. 'Abdu'l-Bahá

93. ibid.

94. ibid.

95. ibid.

96. ibid.

97. "Near-death experience". Wikipedia website. https://en.wikipedia.org/wiki/Near-death_experience

98. Gleanings from the Writings of Bahá'u'lláh. Bahá'u'lláh. CXI p. 216

FURTHER READING

A more comprehensive annotated list of over 60 books and sources can be found in the booklet "Bahá'í Books – A Short Introduction" on Kindle at Amazon.com.

General Books on the Bahá'í Faith

Note: most of the books in this section can also be downloaded free from Bahá'í Ebooks. Or read online at the Bahá'í Reference Library.

Bahá'í Prayers. Bahá'u'lláh. Bahá'í Publishing Trust (US). A compilation of prayers from Bahá'u'lláh, The Báb and 'Abdu'l-Bahá.

Bahá'u'lláh and the New Era. J. E. Esslemont. Bahá'í Publishing Trust (UK). A general introduction. 233 pages.

Book of Certitude: The Kitab-i-Íqán . Bahá'u'lláh. Bahá'í Publishing Trust (US). One of Bahá'u'lláh's most important works which explains prophecies and religion in depth. 237 pages.

Gleanings from the Writings of Bahá'u'lláh. Bahá'u'lláh. Bahá'í Publishing Trust (US). An important selection of passages from Writings of Bahá'u'lláh. 346 pages.

Hidden Words. Bahá'u'lláh. Bahá'í Publishing Trust (US). Profound, gem-like mystical verses revealed by Bahá'u'lláh on the banks of the Tigris. 140 pages.

Introduction to the Bahá'í Faith. A general introduction. 183 pages. Downloadable from the Baha'i Bookstore – Free Downloads (www.bahaibookstore.com).

Paris Talks. 'Abdu'l-Bahá. Bahá'í Publishing Trust (UK). A collection of talks by 'Abdu'l-Bahá in Paris in 1911. 184 pages.

Promise of World Peace, The. The Universal House of Justice. The need for peace and how to achieve it. 1985. Downloadable from https://www.bahai.org/library/authoritative-texts/the-universal-house-of-justice/messages/#19851001_001.

Some Answered Questions. 'Abdu'l-Bahá. Bahá'í Publishing Trust (US). An important compilation of answers to specific questions. 350 pages.

Some Books on the Bahá'í Faith and Life After Death

Close Connections - The Bridge between Spiritual and Physical Reality. John S. Hatcher. Bahá'í Publishing Trust (US). "His latest book explains how the gap between physical and spiritual reality is routinely crossed, and describes the profound implications that result from the interplay of both worlds." 305 pages. Also on Kindle.

Death: The Door to Heaven. Hushidar Hugh Motlagh. Global Publishing. This book shows that we are here for a purpose—a most glorious purpose. 177 pages. Also on Kindle.

In Search of Immortality. Geoffrey Gore. Bahá'í Publishing Trust (US). "...this book explores the journey of life from a spiritual perspective and examines the forces that influence us as we prepare ourselves in this world for the next." Also on Kindle.

Life, Death and Immortality: The Journey of the Soul. Compilers: Terrill G. Hayes and others. Bahá'í Publishing Trust (US). A collection of readings, meditations, and prayers from the Bahá'í writings. 150 pages. Also on Kindle.

Light after Death:The Baha'i Faith and the Near-Death Experience. Alan Bryson. Download from https://bahai-library.com/bryson_light_after_death. A comparison of Bahá'í teaching with NDE accounts.

Purpose of Physical Reality. John S. Hatcher. Bahá'í Publishing Trust (US). "The idea of physical reality as a divine teaching device not only prepares us for further progress in the life beyond, it also provides practical advice about how to attain spiritual and intellectual understanding while we are living on earth." 260 pages. Also on Kindle.

Understanding Death - The Most Important Event of Your Life. John S. Hatcher. Bahá'í Publishing Trust (US). A personal exploration of mortality and death, the inevitable journey of human life, and the acceptance of faith. 311 pages. Also on Kindle.

LINKS

The main international site (www.bahai.org) is a beautiful multilingual site with comprehensive content. The Bahá'í Reference Library (www.bahai.org/library/authoritative-texts/) has the Bahá'í Writings in online and downloadable format. It is the authoritative online source of Bahá'í writings.

Some sites for various national Bahá'í communities:
1. Brazil (www.bahai.org.br/)
2. Canada (www.bahai.org.ca/)
3. Germany (www.bahai.org.de/)
4. India (www.bahai.org.in/)
5. South Africa (www.bahai.org.za/)
6. United States (www.bahai.org.us/)
7. UK (www.bahai.org.uk/)

Some Youtube channels:

1. Official Bahá'í Youtube channel (www.youtube.com/c/TheBahá'íFaith)
2. Official US Bahá'í Youtube channel (www.youtube.com/c/usbahaifaith)

Various other popular sites:

1. Bahá'í World News Service (news.bahai.org)
2. Bahá'í International Community (BIC) (www.bic.org/

documents-and-news-s) – represents the Bahá'í community at the United Nations

3. Bahá'í Blog (www.bahaiblog.net) - a website with a lot of articles, videos, podcasts and photos. Also has a YouTube channel

4. Bahá'í Teachings (www.bahaiteachings.org) – has hundreds of good introductory articles

5. Bahá'í Bookstore (US) (www.bahaibookstore.com) – main seller of books in the US

6. George Ronald Publisher (UK) (www.grbooks.com) - major publisher in UK

7. Bahá'í eBooks (bahaiebooks.org) - source of free ebooks

8. Bahá'í Literature & Publication Trust (India) (www.bahaipublishingtrust.in) – main source in India

9. Bahaipedia (bahaipedia.org) - Online Bahá'í encyclopedia.

Accreditation of graphics

Cover Photo by Pixabay

Flowers Photo by John-Mark Smith on Unsplash

Shrine of the Bab Photo by Arash Hashemi on Wikipedia

Universal House of Justice Photo by author

FURTHER INFORMATION

For further information about this series of
booklets please see the author's blog:
Wondering thoughts (ninewonderings.blogspot.com)

The Bahá'í Faith: - A Short Introduction
The Bahá'í Faith: - A Short Introduction for Christians
The Bahá'í Faith: - A Short Introduction for Muslims
The Bahá'í Faith: - A Short Introduction for Hindus
The Bahá'í Faith: - A Short Introduction for Seekers
The Bahá'í Faith: - A Short Introduction for Women
The Bahá'í Faith and the Cosmos - A Short Introduction
Bahá'í Books - A Short Introduction
The Bahá'í Faith and Life After Death

Revised October 2022

Made in the USA
Monee, IL
26 December 2022

23644784R00049